Buildings

Guided/Group Reading Notes
Purple Band

Contents

OXFORD

Introduction

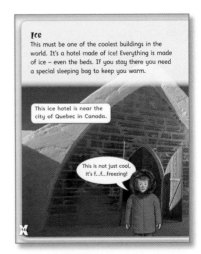

Reading progression in Year 2/Primary 3

In Year 2/P3 children begin to read more
independently using longer texts containing a range
of familiar and unfamiliar vocabulary. Most children are able
to decode new words quickly and automatically, and this helps them
build up their pace, fluency and stamina.

The Project X texts at **purple band** are longer than those at turquoise
band but continue to support children's transition towards greater
independence. They contain a core of familiar high and medium
frequency words and phonically regular words to help build
children's confidence. New vocabulary is introduced within the
context of familiar words and dialogue develops characterisation.
Descriptive vocabulary is used. Throughout the books, natural
sounding language is used as this encourages readers to use their
knowledge of the rhythms and structures of language to support
them as they make sense of the text.

The complexity of character, plot and setting continues to develop,
giving many opportunities for inference and deduction as well as
recall. Longer and more complex
sentences are used at purple band,
so readers will encounter both
compound and complex sentences.
However, there is still a wide range
of simple sentences to support
the reader. A range of punctuation
is used including speech marks
and apostrophes for contraction
and possession.

A range of non-fiction features
including charts, maps,

instructions, labelled diagrams, captions, index and glossaries are used to encourage children to read and interpret information presented in a variety of ways.

Visual literacy is supported through additional information in the illustrations and photographs, and the suggestions for visualization comprehension strategies suggested in these notes.

Progression in the Project X character books

In this cluster, the children continue to use the shrinking power of the watches to explore two settings: in *The Snow Den,* the children build themselves a micro-igloo and experience being inside it; while in *Sandcastle*, Max and Tiger explore the inside of a sandcastle, but become trapped when Molly, Max's sister, fills the moat with water. They escape by climbing aboard a passing flip-flop and surfing back to shore!

Guided/group reading

The engaging content and careful levelling of Project X books makes them ideal for use in guided/group reading sessions. The advantages of using guided/group reading, as well as charts to help you assess the appropriate level for a reading group, are discussed in the *Teaching Handbook* for Year 2/P3.

To use the books in guided/group reading sessions, you should select a book at a band that creates a small degree of challenge for the group of pupils. Typically, children should be able to read about 90% of the book unaided. This level of 'readability' provides the context for children to practise their reading and build reading confidence. The 'challenge' in the text provides opportunities for explicitly teaching reading skills.

These *Guided/Group Reading Notes* provide support for each book in the cluster, along with suggestions for follow-up activities. At purple band, the set of notes for each book could form one or two guided/group reading sessions.

Speaking, listening and drama

Talk is crucial to learning. Children need plenty of opportunities to express their ideas through talk and drama, and to listen to and watch the ideas of others. These processes are important for building reading engagement, personal response and understanding. Suggestions for speaking, listening and drama are given for every book.

Within these *Guided/Group Reading Notes* the speaking and listening activities are linked to the reading assessment focuses.

Building comprehension

Understanding what we have read is at the heart of reading. To help readers become effective in comprehending a text the *Guided/Group Reading Notes* contain practical strategies to develop the following important aspects of comprehension:

- Previewing
- Predicting
- Activating and building prior knowledge
- Questioning
- Recalling
- Visualizing and other sensory responses
- Deducing, inferring and drawing conclusions
- Determining importance
- Synthesizing
- Empathizing
- Summarizing
- Personal response, including adopting a critical stance.

The research basis and rationale for focusing on these aspects of comprehension is given in the *Teaching Handbook* for Year 2/P3.

Reading fluency

Reading fluency combines automatic word recognition, reading with pace, and expression. Rereading, fluency and building comprehension are linked together in a complex interrelationship, where each supports the other. This is discussed more fully in the *Teaching Handbook* for Year 2/P3. Opportunities for children to read aloud are important in building fluency and reading aloud to children provides models of expressive fluent reading. Suggestions for purposeful and enjoyable oral reading and rereading/re-listening activities are given in the follow-up activities to guided/group reading and in the notes for parents on the inside cover of each book.

The Project X *Interactive Stories* software can be used to provide a model of reading fluency for the whole class and/or opportunities for individuals or small groups of children to listen to stories again and again. Listening to stories being read is particularly effective with EAL children. The title *Sandcastle* from this cluster is included on the Year 2/P3 CD-ROM.

Building vocabulary

Explicit work on enriching vocabulary is important in building reading fluency and comprehension. Repeatedly encountering a word and its variants helps it become known on sight. The thematic 'cluster' structure of Project X supports this because words are repeated within and across the books. Suggestions for vocabulary work are included in these notes. The vocabulary chart on pages 10 and 11 lists both decodable and challenging vocabulary for each book and also indicates those words that can be used to support learning alongside a structured phonics and spelling programme.

Developing a thematic approach

Helping children make links in their learning supports their development as learners. All the books in this cluster have a focus on the theme **Buildings**. A chart showing the cross-curricular potential of this theme is given in the *Teaching Handbook* for Year 2/P3, along with a rationale for using thematic approaches. Some suggestions for cross-curricular activities are also given in these notes, in the follow-up suggestions for each book.

In guided/group reading sessions, you will also want to encourage children to make links between the books in the cluster. Grouping books in a cluster allows readers to make links between characters, events and actions across the books. This enables readers gradually to build complex understandings of characters, to give reasons why things happen and how characters may change and develop. It can help them recognize cause and effect. It helps children reflect on the skill of determining importance, as a minor incident or detail in one book may prove to have greater significance when considered across several books.

Note that the books in this cluster can be read in any order. (In some clusters, the 2-part character stories do have to be read in a specific order.)

In the **Buildings** cluster, some of the suggested links that can be explored across the books include:
- finding the location of significant buildings using maps **(Geography)**
- designing and constructing buildings from junk materials **(Art and design)**
- investigating number patterns by building towers **(Maths)**
- adding simple circuits to create lights for model lighthouses. **(DT)**

Reading into writing

The Project X books provide both models and inspiration to support children's writing. Brief suggestions for relevant, contextualized and interesting writing activities are given in the follow-up activities for each book. These include both short and longer writing opportunities. The activities cover a wide range of writing contexts so writers can develop an understanding of adapting their writing for different audiences and purposes.

The Project X *Interactive Stories* software contains a collection of writing frames and 'clip art' assets from the character books – characters and settings – that children can use in their writing.

Selecting follow-up activities

The *Guided/Group Reading Notes* give many ideas for follow-up activities. Some of these can be completed within the reading session. Some are longer activities that will need to be worked on over time. You should select those activities that are most appropriate for your pupils. It is not expected that you would complete all the suggested activities.

Home/school reading

Books used in a guided/group reading session can also be used in home/school reading programmes.

Before a guided/group reading session the child could:

- Read the first few pages – the guided/group reading session then begins at the next unread page
- Read a related book from the cluster to build background knowledge.

Following a guided/group reading session, the child could:

- Reread the book at home to build reading confidence and fluency
- Read the next chapter in a longer book
- Read a related book from the cluster.

Advice for parents on supporting their child in reading at home is provided in the inside covers of individual books. There is further advice for teachers concerning home/school reading partnerships in the *Teaching Handbook* for Year 2/P3.

Assessment

During guided/group reading, teachers make ongoing assessments of individuals and of the group. Reading targets are indicated for each book and you should assess against these reading targets. You should select just one or two targets at a time as the focus for the group. The same target can be appropriate for several literacy sessions or over several texts.

Readers should be encouraged to self-assess and peer-assess against the target/s.

Further support for assessing pupils' progress is provided in the *Teaching Handbook* for Year 2/3.

Continuous reading objectives and ongoing assessment

The following objectives will be supported in *every* guided/group reading session and are therefore a *continuous* focus for attention and assessment (**AF1**). These objectives are not listed in full for each book but as you listen to individual children reading you should undertake ongoing assessment against these decoding and encoding objectives:

- Read independently and with increasing fluency longer and less familiar texts **5.1**
- Know how to tackle unfamiliar words that are not completely decodable **5.3**
- Read and spell less common alternative graphemes including trigraphs **5.4**
- Read high and medium frequency words independently and automatically **5.5**

Further objectives are provided as a focus within the notes for each book.

Correlation to the specific objectives/guidelines within Scottish, Welsh and Northern Irish curricula are provided in the *Teaching Handbook* for Year 2/P3.

 ## Recording assessment

The assessment chart for the **Buildings** cluster is provided on page 45 of the *Teaching Handbook* for Year 2/P3.

 ## Diagnostic assessment

If an individual child is failing to make good progress or he or she seems to have a specific problem with some aspect of reading you will want to undertake a more detailed assessment. Details of how to use running records for diagnostic assessment and resource sheets for undertaking such assessments are given in the *Teaching Handbook* for Year 2/P3.

 **Vocabulary chart**

At Year 2/P3, the children should:

- read high and medium frequency words independently and automatically
- read and spell
  - less common alternative graphemes
  - compound words and polysyllabic words
  - suffixes and prefixes.

NB There are too many common high frequency words in each book to list them all. The first 100 words are known by this stage. A selection is given from the final 200 words in the *300 common words in order of frequency* list. Examples only are given in each category.

Sandcastle	High frequency words	place, over, water, more, something
	Phonetically regular compound and polysyllabic words	sandcastle, explore, amazing, seaweed, tunnel, slippery, retreat, flip-flop, exclaimed, ramparts
	Suffix: -ing	amazing, happening, paddling, soaking, holding, snapping
	Alternative graphemes	/oo/ (ou, ough): through, soon, whooped, you
	Challenge vocabulary	bridge, castle, coloured, built, through
The Snow Den	**High frequency words**	away, over, small, head, soon, around, could
	Phonetically regular compound and polysyllabic words	perfect, snowball, doorway, igloo, stumbled, window
	Suffix: -ly	really, quickly, easily
	Alternative graphemes	/ee/ (ie): squeezed, piece, deep, teeth /ow/ (ou, ough): now, how, ground, found, plough
	Challenge vocabulary	broken, ice, dangerous, building, dome, holes

Cool Buildings	High frequency words	many, much, more, most, live, think
	Phonetically regular compound and polysyllabic words	skyscraper, taller, tallest, earthquake, Empire, factory, prison, fortress, discovered, robot, nicknamed
	Suffix: -ly	friendly, recently, environmentally
	Alternative graphemes	/s/ (ss, c, ce): stone, fortress, city, ice, recently, space
	Challenge vocabulary	skyscraper, Taipei Tower, Taiwan, Burj Dubai, typhoon, Gherkin, Egyptian, Alexandria, Saqqara, Calico, Mojave desert, California, armoury, Bangkok, Thailand, Ohio,
Mr Grim's Tower	High frequency words	dark, best, shouted, found, people
	Phonetically regular compound and polysyllabic words	seagulls, haircut, cheerful, everyone, paintbrush, lighthouse, window
	Words ending in -le	people, hustle, bustle, middle, little
	Alternative graphemes	/ai/ (ai, ay, a-e): paint, sail, sailors, away, day, change, shave, awake
	Challenge vocabulary	hustle, bustle, friendly, countryside
Building Wembley	High frequency words	everyone, best, work, been
	Phonetically regular compound and polysyllabic words	digger, concrete, electricians, bricklayers, football, landmark, floodlights, trenches, mortar
	Words ending in -ed	played, cramped, included, knocked, poured, joined, lifted
	Alternative graphemes	/ai/ (ai, ay, a-e): rain, stay, save, away, crane, safe
	Challenge vocabulary	building, design, stadium, huge, electricity, cables, metres, materials, queues

Sandcastle

BY JAN BURCHETT AND SARA VOGLER

About this book

Max and Tiger are at the seaside with Max's mum and his sister, Molly. They come across a sandcastle and decide to explore it by using powers of shrinking. However, they become trapped when Molly starts filling the moat with water and the only way out is for them to ride on a flip-flop back to shore.

You will need

- *Phoneme and grapheme hunt* Photocopy Master 20, *Teaching Handbook* for Year 2/P3
- *Zones of relevance* Photocopy Master 21, *Teaching Handbook* for Year 2/P3

	Literacy Framework objective	Target and assessment focus
Speaking, listening, group interaction and drama	○ Consider how mood and atmosphere are created 4.3	○ We can talk about how the choice of vocabulary creates different moods and atmospheres in a story **AF5**
Reading See continuous reading objectives on page 9	○ Give some reasons why things happen or characters change 7.2 ○ Explain their reactions to texts, commenting on important aspects 8.3	○ We can sometimes spot the reasons why things change in a story **AF5** ○ We can recognize the important parts of a story and how moods and atmospheres are created **AF2/3**

Before reading

*To activate prior knowledge and
encourage prediction*

- Ask the children if they have ever built
  a sandcastle. Where? What was it like?
- Turn to page 3 and talk about the
  features of the sandcastle, relating
  them to features of a real castle.
- In what ways are sandcastles different
  from real castles? (Emphasize size and
  permanence.) (**activating prior knowledge**)

To preview the text

- Look at page 2 and introduce the characters. Which ones
  are the children familiar with?

*To support decoding and word recognition and introduce
new vocabulary*

- Ask children to identify the beach and sandcastle
  vocabulary on pages 4 and 5. Note them on a word wall,
  perhaps around a picture or sketch.
- **Phonic opportunity** Write the word *shell* on the board.
  Tell the children that there are many words in this story
  which have the /sh/ phoneme in them. Invite them to
  comment on how this sound links with the sea. Refer
  them to words such as *washed* (p.18), *crashed* (p.20) and
  pushed (p.21) and the effects of these on the reader.
- You may also wish to point out some of the high or
  medium frequency words or practise decoding some of the
  phonically regular words in this book and listed in the
  vocabulary chart on page 10.

 **During reading**

As a group, read to page 8. As they read:

- Page 6: Draw the children's attention to the dialogue. Model reading it aloud with expression and using appropriate gesture. Invite children to comment on the use of the punctuation – speech marks, exclamation mark and question mark.

- Page 6: In pairs, allow the children to read the dialogue aloud and invite them to comment on how the atmosphere builds excitement.

- Page 7: With reference to the text and the illustration, encourage children to infer what is happening. (**deducing, inferring, drawing conclusions**)

Ask the children to read from page 8 to the end of the book.

- As they read, ask them to remember times and events when the feelings of Tiger and Max change.

- If you have not already done so, ask the children what to do if they encounter a difficult word, modelling with an example from the book if necessary. Ensure they refer back to the beach and sandcastle vocabulary already noted down. Praise children for successfully decoding unfamiliar words.

··>

 After reading

Returning to the text

- Ask for opinions of the story with particular reference to the different atmospheres created through excitement, fear and problem solving.

·······························>

> **Assessment point**
>
> Listen to individual children reading and make ongoing assessments on their approach to tackling new words and their reading fluency. AF1

> **Assessment point**
>
> Can children describe the different atmospheres in the story, by selecting and retrieving information from the text? AF2/3/5

- Give out the *Zones of relevance* Photocopy Master to groups of two or three children. Ask them to cut out the words and place them face down. In turn, each child turns over a card and decides how strongly that word relates to the story and places it in one of the three zones; the more the word relates to the story, the closer to the centre the child should place the word; if he or she thinks it is not relevant, then it should be placed outside the zones. The children then explain why they chose to place the word where they did. Do their partners agree with them?

Building comprehension

- Ask them to look at page 7. Why do Max and Tiger run behind the rock? (**deducing, inferring, drawing conclusions**)

- Read pages 12 and 13. How have the positions of Max and Tiger changed with relation to Max's sister? How would it feel to be in Max and Tiger's position? (**empathizing, predicting**)

- Now look at pages 16 and 17. Can the children shut their eyes and visualize how a crab would appear if they had shrunk to the size of Max and Tiger? (**visualizing**)

- How does the mood of Max and Tiger change when they find the flip-flop? (**determining importance**)

· ·>

Molly did not look like Max's *little* sister any more. She towered over them holding a bucket. There was a loud *SPLOSH!*
"What's happening?" gasped Tiger.
"Molly has put water into the moat," Max said.

Max and Tiger peeked over the wall.
"Where has she gone?" asked Tiger.
"She must have gone to get more water," said Max. "Let's get out of here!"
They slid down the slippery shell steps.

Building fluency

● Ask the children, in pairs, to reread pages 20–21 to each other. Talk about the relative sizes of Max and Tiger to the sea. Discuss the choice of vocabulary used to describe the sea's action and how it creates a certain mood. Compare the sea in this picture to the one on page 22. How does it reflect the mood now?

· ·>

> **Assessment point**
>
> Do they notice the changes of mood and atmosphere created in the story? AF2/3

Building vocabulary

● Tiger and Max give themselves special names on page 11. Can the children spot the alliteration? Can they think of alliterative words to combine with their own names? What is the effect of their vocabulary choice?

● Develop the word wall started earlier to include a range of vocabulary to support the theme.

· ·>

> **Assessment point**
>
> Are children beginning to recognize the effect on mood and atmosphere of a text that can be achieved through vocabulary choice? AF5

● **Phonic opportunity** Give out the *Phoneme and grapheme hunt* Photocopy Master and ask children to find and list words from the book with graphemes that match the /oo/ sound.

Follow-up activities

Writing activities

● Imagine another occasion when Max and Tiger use their watches to make themselves shrink and explore their surroundings. Write about their adventure, including the excitement, coming face to face with danger and how they solve the problem and return to their normal size. **(longer writing task)**

Provide a sand tray and give pairs or small groups the opportunity to work collaboratively to build a sandcastle. Take a series of digital photographs and load them on to a computer. The group can use these to write a series of instructions or other familiar text type captions to accompany them. (**short writing task**)

The sandcastle

Flag

Tower

Ramparts

Tunnel

Moat

Bridge

Other literacy activities

Recreate the story as a role-play in small groups, recording it with a video camera. During playback, encourage children to comment on how atmosphere and mood have been created throughuse of dialogue and action. Reflect on how music or sound effects could be added to enhance the atmosphere. (**speaking and listening**)

Cross-curricular and thematic opportunities

Investigate castles and, if possible, visit a real one. (**History**)

Remind children of the flip-flop that Max and Tiger found. What other kinds of flotsam, found on a beach, might float? (**Science**)

Investigate features of seasides, such as their locations and habitats, adding vocabulary to the word wall. (**Geography, Science**)

Create collages of beach scenes, incorporating details from the book. Children could use these as illustrations for a series of captions to tell the story in their own words. Alternatively, words and phrases could be built up around the pictures. (**Art and design**)

Investigate capacity and/or volume, using Molly's bucket as a stimulus. (**Maths**)

The Snow Den

BY SHOO RAYNER

About this book

The children make a micro-igloo. When they go back outside they have fun sliding on the icy pond without danger of falling in.

You will need

- *Ice danger* Photocopy Master 22, *Teaching Handbook* for Year 2/P3

	Literacy Framework objective	Target and assessment focus
Speaking, listening, group interaction and drama	○ Tell real and imagined stories using the conventions of familiar story language 1.2	○ We can tell our own version of a story which includes a beginning, a middle and an ending **AF2**
Reading See continuous reading objectives on page 9	○ Use syntax and context to build their store of vocabulary when reading for meaning 7.4 ○ Engage with books through exploring and enacting interpretations 8.2	○ We are building our vocabulary by looking at the way words are used in sentences and how that might help us to understand what the author means **AF5** ○ We can show, through acting out, how well we have understood the story and the characters **AF2/3**

Before reading

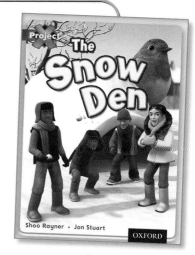

To activate prior knowledge and encourage prediction

- Ask the children if they can remember playing in snow, or sliding on ice. What was it like? (**activating prior knowledge**)

- Look at the cover of the book and talk about the title. What is a snow den? Do they know anything about them? What can they infer from the picture? (**activating prior knowledge, inferring**)

- What might it be like inside a snow den? (**predicting**)

To support decoding and word recognition and introduce new vocabulary

- **Phonic opportunity** Draw children's attention to some of the onomatopoeic words in the text, e.g. *Brrrr* (p.6), *WHOOSH* (p.7), *THUMP* (p.16), *whooping* and *whizzed* (p.17). Talk about the effect of using onomatopoeia and the way the author has placed some words in uppercase letters. Look at the phoneme 'wh'. Check its pronunciation together and begin a collection of 'wh' words.

- You may also wish to point out some of the high or medium frequency words or practise decoding some of the phonically regular words in this book and listed in the vocabulary chart on page 10.

To engage readers and model fluent reading

- Without letting the children see the text, read pages 2 and 3, giving particular attention to the use of speech as a way of differentiating between the characters of Max and Tiger.

- Invite comments about the way the story opens with dramatic action and speech. In pairs, ask children to create two freeze frames to show the action, sharing and making comments, then comparing their ideas with the pictures in the text. (**visualizing and other sensory responses**)

- At the end of page 3, ask the children what are the dangers Max might be thinking about. (**deducing**)

During reading

- If you have not already done so, ask the children what to do if they encounter a difficult word, modelling with an example from the book if necessary. Praise children who successfully decode unfamiliar words.

- Ensure that they understand that sometimes the characters' speech is in speech bubbles.

- Continue to read the story together to page 11.

As the children read, you could ask the following questions:

- Page 9: What is a micro-igloo? Why have the children made the snow den so small?

- Page 10: Why do they turn the dials on their watches? Ensure that everyone understands that the characters have shrunk. (**deducing**, **inferring**)

Ask the children to read to page 21.

- As they read, ask them to think about what it would be like to be one of the characters.

· >

Assessment point

Listen to individual children reading and make ongoing assessments on their approach to tackling new words and their reading fluency. AF1

 After reading

Returning to the text

- Working in pairs, ask the children to retell the story between them with particular reference to the ending. (**recall**, **summarizing**)

· >

Assessment point

Can the children retell the story using appropriate language to make the events of the story flow logically? AF2

Building comprehension

- Would children like to be able to shrink when they play with their own friends? What sort of things would they be able to do if they were tiny? (**visualizing, empathizing**)

- Ask the children to find instances in the story where the reader can infer that the characters are tiny. Refer them to how the characters are able to go inside the small snow den and skate on the sheet of ice. (**deducing, inferring, drawing conclusions**)

- Ask them to close their eyes and imagine what it would be like to be this size and doing these things. (**visualizing**)

· >

Max and Tiger found the broken ice. They dragged a piece back to the igloo.

Max lifted the ice up. Cat and Ant fixed it into the hole. It made a perfect window.

Building fluency

- Look at pages 22–23 and, in pairs, ask the children to retell the story using the pictures for support. (**summarizing**)

- Ask each pair to choose one of the characters to focus on, spending a few minutes together for children to make their choices. Ask the rest of the group to hot seat each pair in turn about the story; each pair answers questions from their character's point of view. If necessary, model how to do this first. (**questioning, synthesizing, empathizing**)

· ⟩

> **Assessment point**
>
> Can children talk about the story, sustaining the viewpoint of their character? AF2/3

Building vocabulary

- **Ⓓ Phonic opportunity** Encourage children to consider the /s/ phoneme which occurs frequently in this text, making the link between the sounds in s*now*, s*lipping*, s*liding* and i*ce*. Comment on the onomatopoeic effect of using this phoneme and compose simple sentences to illustrate this.

· ⟩

> **Assessment point**
>
> Do children understand how the effect of vocabulary choice can influence the meaning for the reader? AF5

Follow-up activities

· · · · · · · · · · · · ·

Writing activities

- Ask the children to write the story of *The Snow Den* from the point of view of their chosen character. (**longer writing activity**)

- Children can plan, act out and then create a comic strip version of their own story about the micro-den. They could create a series of pictures using ICT, adding short captions and simple speech bubbles. (**longer writing task**)

- Complete the *Ice Danger* Photocopy Master. (**short writing task**)

Other literacy activities

- Make a micro-den or igloo using modelling materials. Children can design story boxes to develop speaking and listening skills, and story planning. (**speaking and listening**)
- Use reference books or ICT to find out more about igloos.

Cross-curricular and thematic opportunities

- Investigate how and where traditional igloos were made. (**Geography**)
- Investigate strong shapes for building, such as domes and arches. (**DT**)

- Carry out an investigation into freezing and melting. Put a tray of water in a freezer to make thick and thin sheets of ice. Use these to show the strengths of different thicknesses of ice. (**Science**)
- Make ice pictures by collecting natural materials such as leaves, twigs flowers, floating them in water and then freezing them. (**Art**)

Cool Buildings

BY MICK GOWAR

About this book

This non-fiction text describes buildings of different and unusual shapes, sizes, designs and ages, including buildings made from unconventional materials, such as ice. It also provides facts about why each building is considered special.

You will need

- *Which buildings are the coolest?* Photocopy Master 23, *Teaching Handbook* for Year 2/P3

	Literacy Framework objective	Target and assessment focus
Speaking, listening, group interaction and drama	○ Listen to each other's views and preferences, agree the next steps to take and identify contributions by each group member **3.3**	○ We can work together so that everyone has a chance to share their ideas about the book with the rest of the group **AF2/3**
Reading See continuous reading objectives on page 9	○ Draw together ideas and information from across a whole text, using simple signposts in the text **7.1** ○ Explain organisational features of texts, including alphabetical order, layout, diagrams, captions, hyperlinks and bullet points **7.3**	○ We know how to use a non-fiction book to find out things, without having to search through every page **AF2** ○ We can use the range of features in a text to help us understand it **AF2/4**

Before reading

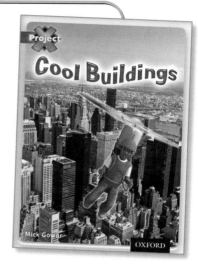

To activate prior knowledge and encourage prediction

- Ask the children if they have ever seen a tall, an old or a strange building. (**activating prior knowledge**)
- Talk about what can be seen in the view of London on pages 2 and 3. Do the children know any of the buildings? Encourage comparison between old and new, tall and small, familiar and unfamiliar.
- Invite suggestions as to what sort of book this one might be. (**predicting**)

To preview the text

- Turn back to the contents page and ensure everyone understands how it supports the way the book can be used; that is, the text does not have to be read in a linear way.
- Ask the children to find the heading associated with page 24, turn to that page, then explore how these features (glossary and index) support the text.
- Can children explain the differences between the three features – contents, glossary and index? (**previewing**)

To support decoding and word recognition and introduce new vocabulary

- Ask the children to choose one word from the glossary that they do not know, read the definition and then share their word and understanding of it with a partner.
- Explore tricky vocabulary such as the building and place names, e.g. the *Gherkin*, *Taipei* and *Alexandria*. Encourage the children to make meaningful associations.
- You may also wish to point out some of the high or medium frequency words or practise decoding some of the phonically regular words in this book and listed in the vocabulary chart on page 11.

During reading

- Tell the children that you want to find out about very large buildings. Model how to refer to the Size section on the contents page, turning to pages 4 and 5, then scanning these pages, perhaps by looking at the picture or the fact box before reading the text. Model the thought processes a reader might have as they read the page, including the raising of further questions.

- Invite children to do the same with the following spread on pages 6 and 7. (**synthesizing**)

- Ask the children to find out about a building made of ice. Set a time limit.

- As they read ask them to think about whether or not they would like to stay in this building and whether they think it is a good material for a building.

⋯⋯⋯⋯⋯⋯⋯⋯⋯⋯⋯⋯⋯⋯⋯⋯⋯⋯⟩

- If you have not already done so, ask the children what to do if they encounter a difficult word, modelling with an example from the book if necessary. Praise children who successfully decode unfamiliar words.

⋯⋯⋯⋯⋯⋯⋯⋯⋯⋯⋯⋯⋯⋯⋯⋯⋯⟩

Assessment point

Do children realize that it is not necessary to read the text in a linear way to find the information they need? AF2

Assessment point

Listen to individual children reading and make ongoing assessments on their approach to tackling new words and their reading fluency. AF1

This is the *Empire State Building*. It took 3400 people one year to build.

New York City in America is full of skyscrapers. The most famous skyscraper is the Empire State Building. It is 491 metres high. It is the tallest building in New York City.

Help!

I'll save you!

The Empire State Building has appeared in lots of films. One of the most famous films was *King Kong*. In the film, a giant ape called *Kong* climbs to the top of the building.

After reading

Returning to the text

- Ask how children located the information about the ice hotel. Discuss how the reader can use the contents page or the index to select sections efficiently and quickly, acknowledging that sometimes readers might just want to browse the book.
- Invite discussion as to the methods used.

· >

Building comprehension

- What do the children think about staying in a hotel made of ice? Would they like it or not and why? Encourage them to infer the conditions from the text. (**visualizing and other sensory responses, deducing, inferring, drawing conclusions**)
- How does the information on the page, other than the main text, support their ideas?
- What other questions does this section raise for them? (**questioning**)

· >

Ice
This must be one of the coolest buildings in the world. It's a hotel made of ice! Everything is made of ice – even the beds. If you stay there you need a special sleeping bag to keep you warm.

Every year the ice hotel melts. So every year it has to be built again. There are 37 bedrooms in the hotel. It is made from about 500 tons of ice and 15 000 tons of snow! Every time it is built, it looks different!

This ice hotel is near the city of Quebec in Canada.

This is not just cool, it's f...f...freezing!

Inside the ice hotel.

27

Building fluency

- In pairs, ask each partner to challenge the other to find out about another type of building. Allow a few minutes for independent reading to identify what they will set their partner to find. Encourage them to be clear in their request and, after an appropriate time allocation, allow children to feed back to each other and then to the group.

· ➤

Building vocabulary

- Locate the words *Billions* (p.2) and *million* (p.11). Clarify their literal meaning in this context.

- Look at *Millennium* (page 12), establish that it means 'thousand' and invite links with other 'milli' words, such as 'millimetre' and 'millipede'.

- Can they find other words that are to do with size, weight or quantity?

Follow-up activities

Writing activities

- Take a wide-angled photograph (or acquire one) of your local area and enlarge it. Invite children to compose the captions to accompany the photograph. (**short writing task**)

- Put together a book of local 'cool buildings'. As a group decide and allocate the contents, with individual authors selecting key words for the glossary and index. Alternatively, create a 'cool buildings' presentation using presentation software. (**longer writing task**)

- Following further research and role play activities, write a story which has a 'cool building' as its setting. (**longer writing task**)

- Complete the *Which buildings are the coolest?* Photocopy Master. (**short writing task**)

Cross-curricular and thematic opportunities

- Invite children to draw a 'cool building' and, if possible, construct it from junk materials. (**Art and design**)
- Challenge children to build a tall, but stable, structure. (**Science, DT**)
- Carry out estimation activities to do with quantity, weight, size and age. (**Maths**)
- Introduce maps to locate significant local, national and international buildings. (**Geography**)

Mr Grim's Tower

BY DAMIAN HARVEY

About this book

This story features Mr Grim – a man with a reputation for being grumpy and grouchy. Fed up with the noise of the town he goes to live in a ruined tower. One day, he decides to have a change and heads off to the barber's, then buys some paint to brighten up his tower.

You will need

- *Mr Grim's thoughts* Photocopy Master 24, *Teaching Handbook* for Year 2/P3
- *Comparatives and superlatives* Photocopy Master 25, *Teaching Handbook* for Year 2/P3

	Literacy Framework objective	Target and assessment focus
Speaking, listening, group interaction and drama	○ Explain ideas and processes using imaginative and adventurous vocabulary and non-verbal gestures to support communication 1.3	○ We can explain our idea about the story, including using gestures **AF2/3**
Reading See continuous reading objectives on page 9	○ Explore how particular words are used, including words and expressions with similar meanings 7.5	○ We can talk about the way the author has used different words with similar meanings **AF5**
	○ Engage with books through exploring and enacting interpretations 8.2	○ We can show understanding of the story and how the author uses effects to create a character **AF2/3/6**

Before reading

To activate prior knowledge and encourage prediction

- Ask the children what the word 'grim' means. Can they show a 'grim' face? Can they use their hands and body posture to show its meaning? (**visualizing**)

- Look at the cover of the book followed by the title page. What do they think the character of Mr Grim will be like? Note down their suggestions. (**predicting**)

- Can they think of any 'grim' characters from other stories?
  (**activating prior knowledge**)

To support decoding and word recognition and introduce new vocabulary

- Draw children's attention to some of the compound words in this book e.g. *haircut, lighthouse, seagull, paintbrush.* Discuss and model how to break these words down in order to make them easier to decode.

- You may also wish to point out some of the high or medium frequency words or practise decoding some of the phonically regular words in this book and listed in the vocabulary chart on page 11.

To engage readers and model fluent reading

- Read up to page 5 to the group, giving particular attention to the intonation of the speech.

- Explain that you are going to pretend to be Mr Grim and that you would like the children, in pairs, to think of a question that they would like to ask you. When responding, use appropriate facial expressions and gestures.

During reading

- Ask the children to read to the end of the story.
- If you have not already done so, ask the children what to do if they encounter a difficult word, modelling with an example from the book if necessary. Praise children who successfully decode unfamiliar words.
- As they read, ask them to look out for any changes they can spot in Mr Grim.

· ·>

As they read, you could ask the children:

- Page 13: What did they feel about Mr Grim at this point?
- Page 22: Draw attention to the contrast between Mr Grim at the beginning of the story and how he is now. What differences would the children notice in Mr Grim if they were one of the people in the queue coming to visit his tower? Make links with the way the author has used words to show the contrast, e.g. dark and creepy, as opposed to bright and light. (**visualizing, determining importance**)

 After reading

Returning to the text

- Ask for the children's opinions of the story, encouraging them to refer to specific changes in Mr Grim, by giving them prompts as necessary.

· ·>

Building comprehension

- Why do they think Mr Grim is grumpy and grouchy? Do they think he experiences other feelings, such as being lonely? (**empathizing, deducing, inferring, drawing conclusions**)

- Look at page 14–15 again. Explore the idea of looking at yourself in the mirror. (You might like to have a mirror available for children to look at themselves.) What did Mr Grim see apart from his reflection? (**deducing, inferring, drawing conclusions**)

- You may wish children to fill in *Mr Grim's thoughts* Photocopy Master to help them think of vocabulary that reflects Mr Grim's moods in different sections of the book.

Assessment point

Are children able to respond to the character with empathy? Do they understand the effects the author has used to create the character of Mr Grim? AF2/3/6

One day Mr Grim looked in the mirror. He frowned at what he saw. "What a grumpy, grouchy, hairy old man you are," he said. "It's time for a change!"

So the very next day, Mr Grim made up his mind. He went into town for his once-a-year shave and haircut. "That's much better," said Mr Grim and he grinned a little grin.

Building fluency

- Ask children, in pairs, to imagine they are Mr Grim and that you are going to ask them a few questions (relate this to a TV or newspaper interview if you feel this is appropriate). Give them a few minutes to rehearse orally their responses before sharing them with the group. Use a range of higher order questions, such as:
  - What made you change?
  - Would you like to move back to the town?
  - Are there any other names apart from Mr Grin that we could call you?

- Help them to develop their responses by asking them to explain why in each case.

Assessment point

Do children use intonation and gesture to support what they are saying? (Intervene to model, if necessary.) AF2/3

Building vocabulary

- Draw round a child in marker pen on plain paper to create an outline of Mr Grim. Write words and phrases to describe how others see him around the outside of the shape and how he himself feels inside.

- Repeat, writing other words to describe characteristics of Mr Grim's transformation to Mr Grin.

- Encourage children to add other similar meaning words when they think of them, using sticky notes.

Assessment point

Do the children notice how the author has used words of similar meaning to create a certain impression of the character? AF5

Follow-up activities

Writing activities

- Take a series of digital photographs of freeze frames to tell the story in pictures. Laminate them and give them to pairs to order. Children can create their own captions. **(short writing task)**

Outside the barber shop, something gave him an idea. He dashed into Bert's Best Buys. He got some paint. When he got back to his tower, Mr Grim started working.

Mr Grim found a paintbrush. He painted his tower white from top to bottom. "There," said Mr Grim. "Now those seagulls can make as much mess as they like. No one will ever know!"

● Invite children to write about the day they went to visit Mr Grim's lighthouse. (**longer writing task**) (To support storytelling, children could first make a story box in pairs: cut the edges of one side of a shoebox so that it flaps down. Then they make a 3D scene to support the story using small world play characters for Mr Grim/Mr Grin and other characters. Stories can then be rehearsed orally.)

Other literacy activities

● Ask children to cut out the words on the *Comparatives and superlatives* Photocopy Master, then use them to play pelmonism, snap or other games. As an extension, you could ask children to think of comparatives and superlatives for other words with endings other than 'y', e.g. sad; sadder; saddest.

● Take digital photographs of children in role as Mr Grim/ Mr Grin. Identify how the body posture, gestures and facial expressions are different.

● Develop the children's role plays, recording their interviews as either sound or video for a local news broadcast. (**speaking and listening**)

Cross-curricular and thematic opportunities

● Explore the feelings people have, e.g. what makes us feel grumpy? How can we help ourselves (and others) to feel happy? (**PSHE**)

● Invite children to look at themselves in a mirror. What can they see? Not see? Look at examples of self portraits by a famous artist, e.g. Van Gogh. Draw or paint a self portrait. (**Art and design**)

● Make lighthouses from junk materials. Add a simple circuit with components to create a light for the model lighthouses. (**DT**)

● Investigate number patterns by building towers with blocks. (**Maths**)

Building Wembley

BY STEVE PARKER

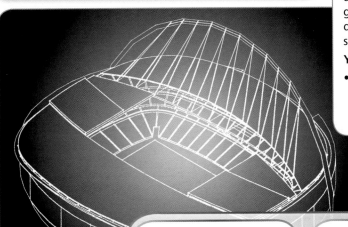

About this book

This non-fiction book describes and illustrates how the new Wembley Stadium was built. It is divided chronologically, giving the before, during and after stages of the stadium's construction.

You will need

- *Building Wembley time line* Photocopy Master 26, *Teaching Handbook* for Year 2/P3

	Literacy Framework objective	Target and assessment focus
Speaking, listening, group interaction and drama	○ Listen to others in class, ask relevant questions and follow instructions 2.1	○ We can listen to each other and ask questions relating to the text **AF2/3**
	○ Ensure that everyone contributes, allocates tasks, and consider alternatives and reach agreement 3.1	○ We can work together so that everyone has a chance to say something about what they have read **AF2/3**
Reading See continuous reading objectives on page 9	○ Draw together ideas and information from across a whole text, using simple signposts in the text 7.1	○ We know how to use a non-fiction book to find out things, without having to search through every page **AF2**
	○ Engage with books through exploring and enacting interpretations 8.2	○ We can explain sections of the text through reading and questioning **AF2/3**

Before reading

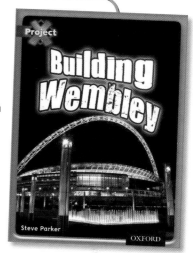

To activate prior knowledge and encourage prediction

- Ask questions to establish whether children recognize Wembley Stadium and know what happens there. Encourage children who know something to respond to questions from the others.
  (**activating prior knowledge**)

- Look at the cover of the book. What can they predict about the contents?
  (**predicting**)

To preview the text

- Look at pages 2–3. Point out the timeline to the children. Allow them to flick through the book to see how it works. Talk about how the book follows a time sequence relating to before, during and after the building of the new Wembley Stadium.

To support decoding and word recognition and introduce new vocabulary

- Begin a word wall with the words *Wembley Stadium* in the middle. Divide the space below it into three sections: *Before, During, After*. Explain that these divisions will help them understand the new words they will meet.

- In the *Before* space write the word 'design'. Establish its meaning, and discuss linking words, such as 'designing' and 'designer'.

- **Phonic opportunity** Challenge children to read some of the longer 2- and 3- syllable words in this book, e.g. *football, bricklayers, electricity*. Support them in breaking these words down in order to decode and blen d the sounds.

- You may also wish to point out some of the high or medium frequency words or practise decoding some of the phonically regular words in this book and listed in the vocabulary chart on page 11.

To engage readers and model fluent reading

- Read to page 9, showing children how to read and relate the captions to the pictures. Model the way that questions are raised in the reader's mind as they read. Add any new words to the *Before* section of the word wall.

- You may wish to read pages 22–23 at this stage, which give general information about the new stadium.

 During reading

- Ask the children to work in pairs (although they will read the text independently). Explain that each pair of children will read four pages between them. (The pages that you want the whole group to read are pages 10–13, 14–17, and 18–21.) Can the group organize and reach agreement as to which pair will read each set of pages?

- As they read, tell them that they will become specialists on that aspect of the building of the stadium and that, after they have read the information, they will tell the others in the group about it and answer their questions.

· ❯

> **Assessment point**
>
> Do children understand that in order to understand their section, it is not necessary to read the sections that come before or after it? AF2

- If you have not already done so, ask the children what to do if they encounter a difficult word, modelling with an example from the book if necessary. These can be added to the word wall. Praise children who successfully decode unfamiliar words.

· ❯

 After reading

Returning to the text

- Remind the children that they are now specialists about different aspects of the building project. Give the pairs a few

> **Assessment point**
>
> Listen to individual children reading and make ongoing assessments on their approach to tackling new words and their reading fluency. AF1

minutes to collaborate on their
understanding of the text they have read.

··>

Building comprehension

- Model appropriate questioning, giving
  examples of retrieval and inferential
  questions. For example, questions for
  pages 8 and 9 could be:
  - Why must the holes be dug?
  - What are they for?
  - When did this take place?
  - What sort of machines were used? (**questioning**)
- Allow time for the same pairs of children
  to think of other questions that people
  might ask about their specialist area.
  (**determining importance, synthesizing**)

··>

Building vocabulary

- As a group, share ideas to add to the word
  wall, bringing together an overview of the
  whole text.

> **Assessment point**
>
> Can children work
> together so that each
> person has a chance to
> say something about the
> text they have read? Do
> they listen to each other
> constructively? AF2/3

> **Assessment point**
>
> Can children work
> together to come up
> with appropriate
> questions? Do they use
> the text to find and/or
> deduce the answers?
> AF2/3

Big holes

Work on the new stadium has
started but it's going down, not up!
First, lots of holes must be dug.

Diggers make long holes
called trenches. These
are for the electricity
cables and water pipes.

BUILDING
WEMBLEY
TIMELINE

2000
2001
2002
2003
2004
2005
2006
2007

These huge holes will be
the rooms and car parks.

To give fans a better view, the new
pitch will be four metres lower than
the old one. There is lots of soil to
take away.

Follow-up activities

Writing activities

- In the pairs that they have been working in, ask children to imagine being a builder working on a particular aspect that they read and talked about. Allow pairs to make a concertina book with captions to show their work. (**longer writing task**)
- Using the *Building Wembley time line* Photocopy Master, ask the children to note down the key activities for each year of construction until the stadium opened. (**short writing task**)
- Prepare a simple presentation about the building of the new Wembley Stadium in pairs. Make *before*, *during* and *after* posters to share with the audience. (**short writing task**)

Other literacy activities

- Invite a builder into the class to talk about their job.
- Create a board game based on the text.

Cross-curricular and thematic opportunities

- Investigate building site opportunities. Create a building site area for small world play. (**Art and design, Maths**)
- Ask the children what their dream stadium would look like. What sports would be played there? Refer back to pages 4–5 and invite children to make a drawing of their own design. (**Art and design**)
- The old stadium was pulled down and the materials were recycled. Find out about recycling and why it is important. (**Science, PSHE**)
- Find out about some of the other countries who have football teams that have played at Wembley Stadium. (**Geography**)
- Play football! (**PE**)